ROCK MY SOUL
CONTEMPORARY QUOTES & WISDOMS

MELISSA REDDING

Bloomington, IN  Milton Keynes, UK

authorHOUSE™

AuthorHouse™
1663 Liberty Drive, Suite 200
Bloomington, IN 47403
www.authorhouse.com
Phone: 1-800-839-8640

AuthorHouse™ UK Ltd.
500 Avebury Boulevard
Central Milton Keynes, MK9 2BE
www.authorhouse.co.uk
Phone: 08001974150

First published by AuthorHouse 11/14/2006

ISBN: 1-4259-1105-6 (sc)
ISBN: 1-4259-1106-4 (hc)

Printed in the United States of America
Bloomington, Indiana

This book is printed on acid-free paper.

DEDICATION

Just wanted to say thanks for showing me the
way;
For grabbing my hand and helping me stand.
Through thick and thin you helped me to bend
Even when I thought it was a sin.
You helped me to see what's locked inside of me.
People should know it may even help them
grow.

Notes from the Author

Allow me to feed your mind with nourishing thoughts, allowing you to enjoy my expressions and receive extreme pleasure from what has been relinquished. And when your soul is full with contentment, allow your mind to hear the repetition of my expressions as they sway your shoulders from side to side as a sign of rejoicing—for I have rocked your soul.

A misunderstood person is someone no one has given any thought to.

❖

When I look at you I know I made the right choice. My heart skips a beat when you kiss me. I don't know if I will ever feel this way again, my child. You're the better part of me.

❖

As I lay here, I know the two of us will never meet again. Once was enough. Now we will go our separate ways. My soul will meet its maker and my body will turn to dust.

All my life I wanted to say,
"Why, Daddy, didn't you stay?"

The human body is a form of art. How creative
can you be with yours?

You can't measure hurt.

Your life is your death and your death is everlasting.

❖

Dreams are created from thoughts. Be careful of your thoughts. They might be dreams.

❖

Why do we have daylight and darkness? Where does the rain and snow come from? Why does the weather change? Who has all power in their hand?

If God is dead, how are we alive?

❖

Scared, hurt, sad—the pain is more than we can bear without faith.

❖

Let me find a word in the dictionary with your face on it.

Always chasing, trying to capture the feelings you had the first time, never stopping to think that's a run you don't need to take. You might not live to enjoy your high.

❖

My mouth is tighter than a sealed envelope.

❖

When you look, do you really see?

Don't displace anger. Make sure the right customer is served.

If I laugh, you smile. If I hurt, you comfort me. If I show my pain, I see your tears. In your absence, I feel your love. You are my friend.

The winds of the heart can blow you down.

I don't care about tomorrow. I've given up on
yesterday.

❖

Think of me like a guitar and let me play your
song.

❖

No reason not to love.
Always there calling my name,
Giving me a thrill.
Oh yeah! I forgot: drugs kill.

If we could turn back the hands of time, what would the clock read?

❖

Don't look at me as if I'm speaking a language you don't understand.

❖

It's the upholstery that tells how strong a relationship is.

You're the closest thing to perfect that I have seen. The only thing that I would change is your last name.

❖

Different doesn't mean bad. It's just one way of being.

❖

My head is saying, "Fool, forget it." My heart is saying, "Don't let go."

Good thing I don't have no thoughts—that means you don't have no food.

❖

She could definitely keep it, but it might itch her to death.

❖

It is easier to face the fear with someone than with no one.

If I die tomorrow, I want to go knowing that I didn't live alone.

❖

You might win some, but you just lost one.

❖

Let the rain wash away my tears, fill my soul, and drown my fears.

The first time was like the sunrise, calm and warm like the earth moving through me. I knew you were the ocean and I was the sand.

❖

A sin is a sin is a sin.

❖

One day I will say goodbye to all I love and who love me. It will be the saddest day—the day my lips will have to say the saddest word: goodbye.

Your kiss touches my soul just as if it is part of me. It's the place I call home.

Nowhere to run,
Nowhere to hide,
No need to lie because the feelings are all inside.

I'll give my life to live again.

Your touch,
Your smell,
The words that you say,
The way you look at me.
No one had to say, "That's your mother."
For I knew the first day.

❖

I held you tight.
Then I pushed you away.
Now I'm asking you to stay.

❖

Mother, don't you know
You are the reason for my love,
My life,
For my being.

Never be afraid to let the world see who you are.
For if the world never sees,
You will never lose your fear.

❖

Don't look back. Look for a better day.

❖

Even if love brings pain, you know that you felt
something.

Tell me why you let it die before I even knew.
Tell me how you could just be through with a
child that you never even knew.

❖

Use what you have to get what you want.

❖

I will close my ears since you won't close your
mouth.

Some say we look alike, that I even act just like
you.
I say, "I don't know that to be true, because I
don't know you."

I know my health cometh from the Lord, whom
I cannot see, but he lives in me.

Brown skin, white skin.
In the end, the color of the skin
Is not the sin.

Love can touch us one time and last a lifetime.

I don't know where to start. Every time I think about it, it hurts my heart. What happened? How did we get so far apart? We used to be young, wild, and free—the best of friends that we could be. Now that I have said my part, where should we start?

I wished I was sitting on top of the world, but the world is sitting on top of me.

Death is as close as life is.

❖

Your mouth is not saying a word, but I hear
everything you're saying.

❖

No end in sight. We are still in a big fight.
Bloodshed, people dead.
I don't know if I have the same view,
But is it worth all we've been through?

I don't carry the name, but I have the blood.

❖

People say it's a miracle, but they never stop to
think where the miracle came from.

❖

As I hold back the tears, I guess I have
something to say.
Why did things happen this way?
We used to laugh and play.
Now all I do is pray, asking the Lord to let you
stay.

Dead presidents rule the world.

There has to be a better place,
Where people are not judged by the color of
their skin,
Where the clouds end and the sun begins,
Where life doesn't stop and love is all we've got,
Where we never have to worry or be in a hurry.

This union I hold dear in my heart.
It's been that way from the very start, never
showing anything but care. Someone is always
there, maybe not under the same roof.
All the love is proof.
My family is all I've got, and to me that's a lot.

By crossing the line, you're crossing me.

❖

My life is confidential material.

❖

When it rains in heavy spurts, the angels in heaven are crying tears of joy, reminding me that you are there.

Don't look at yourself in the mirror to see.
Look inside your soul.

❖

I don't physically fight but I've always had to
fight. Try using your mind.

❖

Love can be a battle and everyone is left with
scars.

Put a stamp on it and send it to someone who cares.

❖

You have captured my attention. Make good use of your time.

❖

Why doesn't my heart follow my head?

Have you closed the road or am I free to drive?

❖

We all need a place where defenses are down
and fear can't be found.

❖

I never believed that life was a precious gift.
How then could it be that I gave birth to thee?

We climb mountains in life. Just remember, once you reach the top it's all downhill.

❖

You're my thief. You stole my heart.

❖

I need you like the air I breathe.

It's warm and safe. I enjoy it more than words can say. I am not there often, but when I am it is peace on earth, knowing that the place I call home still has the same effect on me.

Why do I feel that anything good that happens in life is an accident?

The rain is coming down hard. I need to take cover before my heart drowns.

Don't be a hurricane and make a mess with your life.

❖

The day after is probably one of the hardest days in life. The relationship you once had is no more and the person you long to see will never be.

❖

It's hard to be tender in a world that's so tough.

You're like a drug.

❖

Miracles come if you believe.

❖

Don't be my appetizer. Be my main course.

We all have a reservation we aren't privileged to cancel.

❖

I'll bare my soul if you share your heart.

❖

I'm breathing but I am not alive.

A new horizon needs to come into my view.

❖

Whether you quit or are fired from my union,
you won't be rehired.

❖

When it comes to love, I'm not seasoned.

Emptiness has found me. It won't let go.

❖

Love is blind, but if you want your vision to improve try marriage.

❖

A man will protect his own even if he stands alone. He'll work himself to the bone to make sure he is taking care of home.

It's not just about family. It's about knowing who we are to make sense out of our own lives.

❖

All of us have a story. It's not how we tell it. It's how we live it.

❖

With every beat of my heart, there's a beat for the ones I love.

Be open not closed. Have some ability to comprehend and communicate without being judgmental. Not only will you have heard what was said, but you will have listened.

❖

Struggles are beautiful when we rise above them.

❖

Life shouldn't be a set plan. Life should be about all the possibilities.

We always see people's faults and speak on them. Rarely do we speak of people's accomplishments.

❖

Remember, when your heart is heavy and it seems like all hope is lost, this too shall past.

❖

Life can be hella-hella fun or just hell.

Time will steal your life.

❖

Relationships are emotional bank accounts.
Don't just always make a withdrawal;
sometimes make a deposit.

❖

Our state of mind allows us to feel. Our feelings
don't allow us to force our state of mind on
someone else.

If you're always crying the blues and things aren't getting better, maybe you should dry your eyes and believe a change is gonna come.

❖

Open eyes still travel blind.

❖

Not asking and not listening, we miss out on a lot.

I'm still standing.

❖

The world is a circle of life.

❖

Sometimes we have to let our concerns be like a breeze: through our fingers and slip away.

Life is about phases. I'm ready for the next one.

❖

Finding something that you love is a million times better than finding something that makes you rich.

❖

You promised me heaven but you have put me through hell.

Money buys choices.

❖

You're my *Juicy Fruit* that gives me *Good 'n'
Plenty.* You're my superstar and my *Million
Dollar Bar.* You're my almond that brings me
Joy. Your financial status isn't what matters, as
long as you receive a *Pay Day.* You helped me
to fight my battles because you are a *Musketeer.*
My life was hard before you. Now I enjoy the
Milky Way. I sure hope that you will stay.

❖

Most people are sorry for the things they have
said. I'm sorry for not saying what I needed to
say. Now I have to rely on time to heal my heart.

When the mountain won't move, stand on it.

❖

Life can be full of work or you can work to have
a full life.

❖

Take what you need in this world. Just
remember to give what you can.

You can't help what you are anymore than you can help what you aren't.

❖

Sometimes we have so many distractions that the distractions start to become distractions from the distractions.

❖

Life is simple. People make it complicated.

Knowing your heritage allows you to know who you are, to a certain degree. You still need to know what's in your heart.

❖

Yesterday's blues need to be yesterday's news. Throw it away and sail on!

❖

Some answers to questions don't come from your mental state of mind. They come from your heart.

Sometimes when you're trying to collect your thoughts, it's as if your mind becomes a television—always changing channels.

❖

Never get caught up in thinking that not speaking of a problem means there isn't one.

❖

The mind's eye shows things that the natural eye just can't visualize.

Hide-and-seek is a childhood game. Yet for some adults, they hide who they are in hopes that no one will be able to seek out who they truly are.

❖

People don't make us who we are. They add to it so the package is complete.

❖

Seek and you shall find only applies when you know what you're searching for.

We all fall. Just don't fall apart.

❖

Storms come and we complain. Blessings come
and we forget to say thank you.

❖

Here's a clue: the only way out is through.

Nowadays, people don't want relationships.
They want to be free agents.

Treat your life like it's a project. Never stop
working to make it better.

Society won't allow some stains to be washed
off.

You're the wind beneath my wings. You're my beacon in the night. I look to the hill to find my health. I'll be forever grateful. I'm everything. I am because you created me.

❖

When a line is formed, it shouldn't matter where you are standing in line. You should be concerned with what line
you're in and your reason for standing in the line.

❖

Up yonder is the last stop on my journey.

Sometimes we have to weep to move on.

❖

There are times when being in denial is just one step from being stupid.

❖

Pursue excellence by any means necessary.

I ain't her!

❖

Yesterday I cried. Today my soul is open. Tomorrow I pray I will have hope and strength.

❖

Always have an internal spot where there's a state of calmness and quiet so that when life gets to be overwhelming you can go to that place and have peace and serenity.

Some abilities that people have aren't explainable nor do we understand. Maybe they should be viewed as a gift from a higher power.

❖

I met you at your death, a grown woman feeling like a lost and lonely child: too scared to move, too angry to cry, but all the time wondering how someone who gave life didn't want to share life.

❖

Life gets more precious when there's less of it to waste.

You can't look for happiness through anyone but yourself.

❖

Other than my skin, your friendship is the closest thing to me.

❖

I didn't see the rain coming. Now my life is having a major flood.

Sometimes anger can make you want to reach out and touch.

❖

Sometimes we have to remodel our lives.

❖

Sometimes life makes us feel like queens or kings of sorrow.

You're no longer here, but you're still in my heart.

There was a time when I heard your voice and my mouth would form a smile. There was a time when your touch would send my heart racing. There was a time when your eyes told stories that only I could read. The way I loved you then is the way I hate you now.

Poetry is in motion every time we look at the wonders of the world.

For some, there are partners in life. For others, it's a lifetime of partners.

❖

Love finds its own way.

❖

People are works in progress. Just remember each person works different hours.

With each day a little rain must fall. Without it
we would not grow.

Some people can't totally conform to society
because they don't feel like they are a part of it.

If someone were to ask me how long I am going
to love you, I would have to say: until the end of
time.

Life doesn't treat you like Burger King. You won't always have it your way.

❖

Why can't the whole human race have what they deserve: freedom, justice, and equality?

❖

People are like blue jeans.
The longer you wear them,
the more comfortable you become.

Always sing your own song, even if you're singing out of key.

❖

Empty spaces can fill you full of holes.

❖

Life won't allow you to be a hitchhiker. There are no free rides.

When you're searching for a soul mate, pray that one will be sent who lost his or her way from heaven.

❖

Just because we don't speak the words doesn't mean we don't feel the feelings.

❖

There's no rewind in life. The scene is just a roll.

Whatever the Master is going to do for you, he has to do it through you.

❖

Acting crazy is being fun loving. Being insane is being crazy.

❖

We need to treat our problems like our clothes and iron them out.

You truly are the best,
miles above the rest.
You move like the desert wind.
You have to be a sin.

❖

Being in a bad storm doesn't mean that you
won't come out clean on the other side.

❖

Life experiences will make you transform.

People that we care about can sometimes make us feel like we're drowning in a sea of love.

❖

The King restores my soul because I believe in him. Yet I fear what I don't understand and what may be unexplainable.

❖

I would like to think that everyone has a little hero in them, because I pray that everyone has the courage to do something positive and good.

Folks say, "You can't miss what you haven't
had."
That's really sad, 'cause each and every day
I've missed you, Dad.

❖

To feel is natural. To express our feelings is rare.

❖

My soul got happy so I stayed and my world was
rocked.

Do you look at the physical or the soul to see beauty?

❖

If only race was viewed like colors in a box of crayons.

❖

Know what it is you're feeling when you're feeling it.

From day one we are born to live the story that was written for our lives.

❖

We don't have total control without a substance. What makes us think we have any with a substance?

❖

Make sure that you're sure.

Sometimes we have to close our eyes to see clearly.

❖

Time is like a river forever flowing.

❖

If there's a solution to every problem, is there an answer to every question?

Mistakes make us who we are.

❖

Whether you're fighting your own personal battle or fighting a battle for your country, we live in a world of wars.

❖

How much time is there between the womb and the tomb? However much time there might be, it's never enough.

What you see is what you get if you believe everything you see.

❖

Parenting isn't part time or temporary. It's always and forever.

❖

Tomorrow will come, but tomorrow may not be the day you need. But your tomorrow will come.

Meeting expectations is great. Surpassing them is even better.

❖

Everything we do we don't choose. Some things choose us.

❖

We all want love but more important, we all need love.

If heaven is as beautiful as you are, I have already died and gone there.

❖

Life is a game that must be played. There are no winners or losers —only people trying to survive.

❖

Don't allow hate to put you in a state of imprisonment. Love and your soul will always be free.

Your conscience can prosecute you to the point you wish you were in a court of law.

❖

Don't mourn my death. Celebrate my life. Hang on to my memories. Think of me as a flower at the end of the season. I'll bloom again. It just won't be here on earth.

❖

This is your life. Make it one that you can be proud of.

Hopefully, one day love and compassion will be the standard.

❖

Abstaining doesn't lessen one's desire for something.

❖

Giving someone an apology is making a statement. Showing them you're sorry allows them to see your regret for the wrong.

A day without laughter is a day without happiness.

❖

The day will come when we will be absent from the body and free from all restrictions.

❖

Regardless of any and all situations we are blessed.

When opportunity knocks, don't be so quick to answer. See who or what is knocking first.

By underestimating the power of prayer, you might be lacking the belief that He lives.

Sad but true: if there never were stormy weather and cloudy days, how would we know to appreciate the sunshine?

One day I came in. One day I will leave out.
Both ways the creator will travel with me.

❖

You're the producer of your life. Make it a
winning performance.

❖

If the weather was the only thing that turned
cold, the world would be a warmer place.

As our children become adults, it doesn't mean that they're no longer our kids. They will still need our support through life's journey and we still need to be the cream to make their journey as smooth as possible.

You are blessed to have all of your body parts, so don't act like you can't stand for what you believe in. You have a spine.

Unfortunately, there are people in the world that are earth disturbers.

Everyone can fly. All we have to do is believe,
spread our wings, and soar.

❖

Never allow life to steal all your innocence.

❖

Never take more than you give in life.

All men were created equal, but we won't be equal unless we treat each other that way.

❖

Some feelings are great to go through but hell to get over.

❖

Sooner or later we must all sleep alone.

If you find happiness in life, you're successful.

❖

All things will be revealed in time.

❖

Because you're leaning doesn't mean you're not standing.

A mistake doesn't stop the love, but it might make someone walk away.

❖

Work hard today so you can live better tomorrow.

❖

Love is a gift that money can't buy.

Conversation can spread like wild fire.

❖

If it's a mountain, climb the mountain. If it's a
river, cross the river. If it's a bump in the road,
go around it. If it's fear, there's nothing to fear
but fear itself. So meet it head-on. Whatever it
is, don't let it stop you from achieving.

❖

Each day we have a new beginning.

Work through your anger. Don't let your anger work through you.

❖

I pray time will rid us of the pains of the world.

❖

When your life ends, the world will continue on. So make your mark on the world while you have the chance.

Life and love are both a roll of the dice—so don't crap out.

❖

Always be who you are. Never try being someone you're not. Be you and you'll be fine.

❖

Tomorrow is just another day for some, but for the children tomorrow is their future.

What you demand from others you should give in return.

❖

Brilliance comes in hindsight. Wouldn't it be great if the order was reversed?

❖

Sometimes life puts us in rough waters. Don't panic and drown. The waters will calm down.

If you have something to give, give it while you have the chance. Chances don't last forever.

❖

It's your choice. You can swing or hang yourself from a rope.

❖

Don't sweep things under the rug, because the rug will be moved and the dirt will still be there.

You gave my life purpose. You gave me a reason for living. Carrying you in my womb was a great joy, one a mother would only understand. Now I would give my life to be close to you again. Rest easy, my child.

❖

Memories are great to make because we never know when we may be forced to live with them.

❖

When you sleep, remember to let your mind rest.

Always have your rain gear if the forecast is love. Sometimes you'll have to weather the storm.

❖

When you're carrying a load that's too heavy and you don't know where to go, go down on your knees.

❖

Here we are, two adults still playing games. I hide my heart and what do you do but seek it out.

The blessing is having a slice of the pie. Don't try to obtain the whole pie. Take your slice and pass it on.

❖

Your love must be a drug because I'm addicted. Your love is uncut and pure.

❖

Dream your dreams until your dreams come true.

Beauty can't be obtained. It's natural.

❖

Some of us simply need help, while others are simply helpless.

❖

The heart beats with repetition to allow us to know that we're alive,
but the body is an armor to protect the soul.

When we lose someone we love it's like
watching the sun go down.

❖

My victory comes from knowing that I'm not
running this race alone.

❖

Never walk in anyone's shadow. Follow your
own.

Scars allow us to know not only that our past is real but also that we made it through.

❖

Pursue excellence by any means necessary.

❖

Have the wisdom to know that family shouldn't grow apart.

There's danger in all things, so always proceed with caution.

❖

Relationships test our endurance. Make sure you're up for the marathon before you run the race.

❖

Life is a cliff hanger because you never know what's going to happen from one moment to the next.

If you want to improve your looks just smile.

❖

When you love someone, you carry them in your spirit.

❖

When you love somebody, you should tell them and trust that they won't abuse the information.

A fool for love sometimes can be a fool for pain.

❖

There's always a hole in the wall. It's called a door. Sometimes we have to use it.

❖

A child is the strongest hope for the future. We need to save the children so the nation will continue to grow.

If you're human, you won't walk a perfect step through life.

❖

You get what you give.

❖

The loads that we carry are the loads that we are supposed to bear.

Never allow your heart to live as a hermit. Share it and feel the joy of love.

❖

Sometimes it is as if men and women come from two different hemispheres. We're just miles apart.

❖

In some homes you're not welcomed, but we can dwell in the house of the Lord forever and ever.

Those who know the least always seem to say the most.

❖

How close is too close?

❖

My wish is to be free from all the hurt and pain that life has to offer. I want to be free to feel the happiness in the days I have left.

Know the difference between glass and diamonds. If you're lucky enough to find a diamond, treat it well and let the beauty of the relationship come shining through.

❖

Great loves are like achievements. They both involve great risks.

❖

We need to get back to bowing our heads to pray, asking family to stay, and showing people the way.

Have we overcome?

❖

Touching one soul at a time can start a revolution.

❖

Somebody is out there somewhere.

There is no changing direction or missing your turn. We each have to drive solo. The lights will flicker then turn dark. There will be no U-turns or any way out on the day we meet our dead end.

❖

Everybody wants me to be what they want me to be.

❖

Driving off the road of life is something that naturally happens, but the further off the road that you travel the harder it is to find the smooth pavement again.

You can't feel what you don't.

❖

Boundaries don't keep people out. They fence
you in.

❖

You can't believe in someone you can't forgive.

Think of dreams as one-way tickets to a better life.

❖

Don't fear change.
Fear things never changing.

❖

A common purpose in life should be happiness.

School will never end.
We attend it every day.
It's called the School of Life.

❖

All expenses in life aren't monetary but they
can be high priced.

❖

When your mind drifts off like smoke, inhale so
you can collect your thoughts.